Praise for **Winning Words, Winning Life**

"*Victoria Draper is a master of words, changing many people's futures in the process, including mine! Being a personal growth coach under Bob Proctor, I can say with confidence the words we speak dictate how we feel and act and therefore our results.*"

– Michael Chocholousek, PGI Consultant

"*When I met Victoria, her words gave me the courage to start living my truth. Her intuition, advice and willingness to share her story with me is just what put me on the path to starting my business by changing my fear into FAITH!*"

– Timmy Rodriquez, Artist

"*Victoria is inspiring! She helped me to grow my choreography business! I had to start turning down clients, because I was so busy! Kudos to Victoria and the power of our words!*"

– Leslie Reed, Professional Dancer / Choreographer

Published by
Hasmark Publishing
www.hasmarkpublishing.com

Permission should be addressed in writing to Victoria Draper at victoria@winningwordswinninglife.com

Editor: Corinne L. Casazza
corinnecasazza@gmail.com

Cover & Book Design: Anne Karklins
annekarklins@gmail.com

ISBN 13: 978-1-989161-61-6
ISBN 10: 1989161618

FAST TRACK TO LIFE SUCCESS

Winning WORDS Winning LIFE

Victoria Draper

To my Gramma,
who always said in sweet broken English, "study da book."
She encouraged my higher education and
supported my desire to be, do and have more in life.

ACKNOWLEDGEMENTS

Thank you to God for this life and all blessings.

Thank you to my family and friends for being a part of who I am and sharing in this life's journey.

Thank you to my teachers, mentors, role models and coaches throughout my life for believing in me and supporting my vision when I needed it most.

TABLE OF CONTENTS

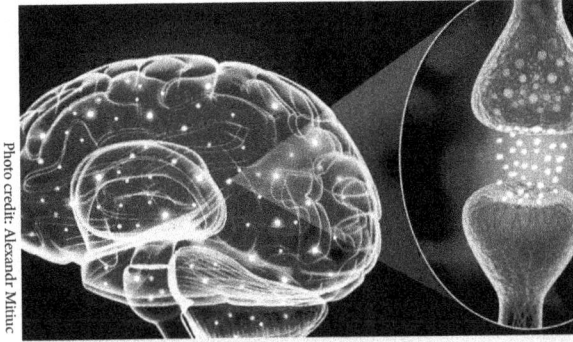

Photo credit: Alexandr Mitiuc

CHAPTER 1

Simple Science

Before we get into how you're going to fast track yourself to your ultimate winning life, there's a concept to understand regarding how our brains work relative to our speech and how this contributes to winning or losing patterns in life. It's called Neurolinguistics.

Neurolinguistics is the branch of linguistics dealing with the relationship between language and the structure and functioning of the brain. There's a practical application of this connection called Neuro-linguistic Programming (NLP), which is an approach to communication, personal development and psychotherapy created by Richard Bandler and John Grinder in the 1970s. There's extensive material on the subject, textbooks and classes at most universities where you can study this. However, I want you to have fast results now, so let's get to the fast track version.

THE BASICS: Everything we do in speech and movement starts as a thought in our brain and is carried out via neurotransmitters through neuropathways. A neurotransmitter is an electrical pulse that transmits a signal in your body for activity. For example, when you snap your fingers, there's first a thought to snap your fingers, then the signal from your brain goes to the muscles in your fingers to make them snap, and your fingers complete the requested motion. So, there's literally a pathway from your brain to your fingers along which these neurotransmitters travel to carry out the command from your brain.

Neurotransmitters then transmit feedback on the resulting action back to the brain so the brain can determine if the command was carried out successfully or not and whether an adjustment is needed for better results.

Consider, for example, when you first learned to snap your fingers, probably as a child. Your first attempt might have felt awkward and required tremendous effort and you didn't make a snapping sound. On your second, you took the results from your first try and changed something to create a better snapping sound. The third, you took the results from the second attempt and changed a little more to create a nice crisp snap. However many attempts it took for you to learn, once your brain figured out what's required to make the snapping sound, you were able to do it easily without much thought or effort and the result was pristine thereafter. The neurotransmitters did their job and formed a strong neuropathway after some repetition and now it's a learned skill.

The point is that neuropathways get stronger with repetition. If it's an intentionally learned skill like snapping your fingers, it becomes easier and more automatic and that feels good and comfortable. On the flip side, if you unintentionally picked up a bad habit, the more you've repeated that habit, the same applies and that's why it's hard to break. The pathway is strong. It might even feel good carrying out old bad habits because it's familiar and easy to do something you've always done.

Now consider how this is true for speech patterns as well. For some, it's hard to imagine why words are subject to the same principles because words are just sounds, right? No, they're more than that. Your tongue is a muscle and your tongue forms different shapes to create different sounds and words.

Let's take this to the next level of awareness, and recognize that in addition to the words we use to express ourselves outwardly, there are the words we say silently to ourselves. Our thoughts are silent words. They're the conversation we have with ourselves and what we believe about ourselves, which plays a role in our success in life. So, in this material, we'll address and correct the ins and outs of successful communication to ensure you find your winning words and winning life.

What we're doing here is mastering our minds, ourselves and our life with our words.

EXERCISE

Get a sheet of paper and write a numbered list of things you'd like to improve in your life. These things can be about anything. Then go through it and read your list one item at a time. After every item say, "yes, I want this," aloud and set the list aside for future reference. As you go through the book and learn techniques and tools to change your word choice for the better, come back to this list and rewrite the statements one at a time (at your own pace) in new ways to produce better results.

CHAPTER 2

Speech Habits

Speech habits, like saying "um" a lot, are just patterns formed at some point unconsciously. The pattern is repeated constantly so now it happens automatically and without you noticing – until you see yourself in a video or something.

The characteristics of speech are also habits. Your volume, speed, pitch, and more. Even the content and quality are habits. The things you tend to talk about and whether they're oriented in a positive or negative light are also habits.

We learned most of our patterns at a young age from our families, community, teachers, coaches and everyone in our environment. At the earliest age, we begin mimicking everyone around us, starting with sounds, then words, sentences and styles.

If we learned good manners early on like saying "please" and "thank you" then that's a pattern. Equally true, any poor behavior we learned is also a pattern. As children, we don't actively filter who we listen to and who we copy. We're like a sponge and copy everything until we're aware enough and able to choose something different for ourselves.

The reason to choose better words and thoughts is to see better results in our life. Think of the inspirational stories of athletes with obstacles stacked against them who end up a leader or superstar or sports hero. At some point, they decided to tell themselves "yes I can" and believed they could achieve their goals. They practiced doing so more and more. They repeated positive words and actions and developed strong neuropathways that led to their success. Their success was not by accident, it was based on the dominant thoughts, speech and actions they engaged in.

There are certain qualities of speech and behavior that are found in the majority of great leaders, speakers and super powers in this world. And there's a whole population that seek out training through programs like Toastmasters and speech class or therapy. And all of these are options for you. However, to reiterate, my vision was to bring all that highly sought after programming and information here in one easy format, to eliminate the extensive time and money that some invest to get that winning edge.

These are examples of those who became winners by choice. They chose winning thoughts and words and actions. You can too… and right now. Choose winning.

EXERCISE

Beginning today, create a new habit of pausing for two seconds before responding to any question and before making a statement about anything in your personal and professional life. In this two second pause, take a breath in and out and think "Winning Words." Then proceed with the intention of producing winning results in every area of your life. As you go through the book, you'll learn several techniques that you'll be able to choose from in different situations that best suits the context of your speaking.

CHAPTER 3

Words Trigger Images

Words we speak and hear trigger images automatically and immediately in our mind.

Think of your neighbor telling a story about their dog playing with their kids the other day. While they're describing the scene, you're picturing it and watching it play out like a movie in your mind. You picture their dog running around and the kids laughing. It's automatic. You hear it, you see it.

Now think of a different neighbor that's always talking about accidents and traffic during their work commute and a robbery across town. Again, while they're describing everything, you're running images of those things while they're talking. It's automatic.

This is equally true for things you talk about. While you're telling a friend about a beautiful relaxing weekend you had, you're thinking of everything that happened, the quality time with a loved one, a beautiful sunset and some amazing, tasty margaritas you enjoyed. You're reliving all those details visually in your mind while you're talking. And so is your friend who's listening to you.

Therefore, choosing to talk about things related to the success you want in your life is going to have you playing out images of success in your mind. Choosing to spend time with people who are also talking about things related to success triggers more images in your mind related to success.

The reason this is important is because images are the most powerful element driving your subconscious mind. And your subconscious mind is the most powerful force driving the results in your life.

Thinking again about the athlete who's focused on the end result they want; they talk about it, they think about it and that's why they end up with exactly what they want. Their coach is speaking words of encouragement and that feeds their success. The athlete is hearing those words, they're imagining the positive end result, and their subconscious plays out until they're winning.

Therefore, you must choose words that feed success. Choose words that trigger positive images of success in your mind. Be with people who participate in conversation that is success oriented. Choose winning words, winning images and your winning life.

EXERCISE

Get the list you created during the action item in chapter 1. Go through and highlight the individual words that singularly represent the things you want. For example: If you described a new car that you want, how you'd drive it around, how much you love it and how cool it is, highlight the word "car" in that sentence. Perhaps it's a "truck" or it's a "Range Rover" and you'd highlight those words. If you wrote a paragraph about the vehicle you want, then identify the one word in that paragraph that pinpoints what you want. Repeat this for everything on your list. Then get a new sheet of paper and write a list of the highlighted words for the next chapter and exercise.

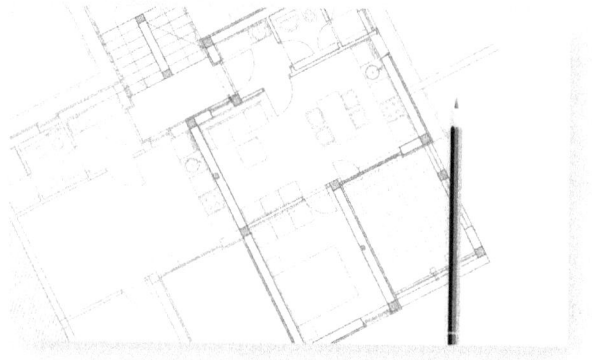

CHAPTER 4

Images Drive Results

"If you can see it in your mind, you can hold it in your hand."

– Bob Proctor

Anything you want in your life must first be a clear picture in your mind. Decide what it is, declare it in words that create a clear image in your mind. Keep speaking in terms of assumed success and keep the clear image in your mind while walking the path consistently and it will happen.

Think of a trip you want to take. For example, taking a ski trip for the weekend. First you say to yourself, "I want to go skiing this weekend." The moment you say that, you picture yourself skiing. Then you picture where you'll stay, how you'll get there, who you'll stay with and when you'll leave home. Then you carry out the steps and make it happen. The point is, you first have to have the clear picture in your mind before you get what you want.

Now say, for example, you had doubts about spending the money for the trip or doubts about the weather or you're not sure where you want to stay or if everyone would cancel on you. If you had thoughts (silent words) and images of all these things going wrong, you might talk yourself out of the trip and not go. You might think this isn't a reasonable route because there's too much risk. In this opposing scenario, the thing to acknowledge is, bottom line, you don't get what you want. You killed the vision before you started.

Most people choose the second route. They talk themselves out of what they really want because they have doubts and fears. They focus on all the negative instead of the positive. Now to be fair, obstacles may appear in planning the ski trip. Maybe something comes up with the car or a friend cancels so you have to find someone else. There are things that will happen in life that are out of your control. However, staying focused on the vision of getting there and having a good time, will get you there. In the opposite case, if you take obstacles as signs to give up on something you want, then of course you won't get what you want.

Keep the image of what you want in mind and it will move towards you while you're moving towards it. Keep choosing words in alignment with your vision. Choose winning words and winning images for winning what you want.

EXERCISE

Get your list of words that you created with the action step in Chapter 3. Now, do a Google search and on each word on your list and capture a screenshot of each item. You can also do this by cutting out images from a magazine, however online searches are easier and faster and we are looking for your fast track, right? Now save all those images in an album on your computer or phone or print them out and make a collage of them. This is now your vision board that you'll look at at least once a day. This gives you something to focus on in your visualizations and help manifest what you want.

Every morning from this point on, spend time looking at your collage and say "yes" to everything you want and feel what it will feel like when you get it.

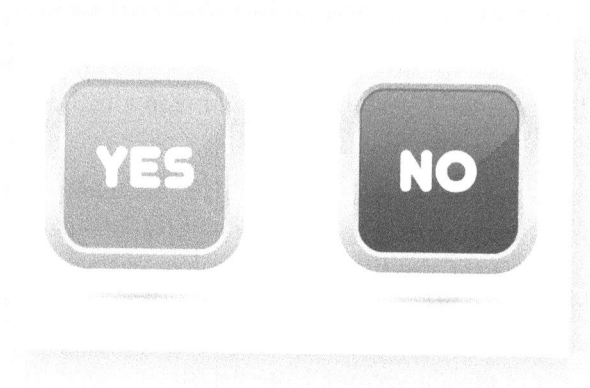

CHAPTER 5

Wants and Don't Wants

Focusing on what you want triggers images in your mind that then trigger your subconscious mind to achieve the desired result.

The same goes for what you say you don't want. So be careful. Negative words you speak trigger images of what you don't want and the subconscious mind obediently manifests what you DON'T WANT. If you say, "I don't want to make a mistake," you're focusing on your fear, triggering your nerves and feeling fear and anxiety. Your anxiety disrupts your nervous system and you manifest the exact thing you say you don't want. Saying what you don't want doesn't make it go away. It magnifies it. It's just the way the mind and body work.

So, focus on what you DO want and let THAT be magnified. Saying "I want a great performance," allows you to think of how things can go well for you. You allow yourself to succeed because you picture yourself confident and clear and performing well. You feel that success and it must play out because you have the image in your mind.

Think about the top athletes in the world and their performance. They have a dialogue going on within them. Probably something like, "I'm going to practice, I'm gonna work on that shot, I'm gonna keep hitting it on the mark, I'm gonna get it right." In a two hour practice, they'll probably miss a lot of shots, however, they make more than they miss. They keep going and make more good shots. And more. They keep thinking of the success and talking success to themselves and following through with shot after shot until they see the consistent successful shots they want. They're thinking of what they want, not what they don't want. Athletes who focus on what they don't want are the ones who choke at the last minute or fall apart when it matters.

Think about the top business success stories of the world. Same thing. Someone had an idea for a business or product and they just focused on the success. They kept going past every obstacle and overcame every challenge because they stayed focused on the end result... success. Focus on what you want. Success.

Apply this principle of focusing on the positive and improve the quality of your life right now. A few examples are:

"I don't want to be late" becomes "I want to be on time."

"I don't want another argument" becomes "I want harmony."

"I don't want to be messy" becomes "I want to be organized."

EXERCISE

Get a sheet of paper and draw a vertical line down the middle. Refer to your original list from chapter 1 if needed for ideas in this exercise. On the left side, list the things you want to improve in the form of "don't want" statements. Then on the right side, write the opposite of that statement, which is what you DO want. For example: if one of the things on your list is improving your financial situation, then your statements might be "I don't want to have limited income anymore" and then you would craft something like "I want to enjoy multiple sources of regularly increasing income from doing things I like."

Yes, I CAN.

CHAPTER 6

Affirmations

Affirmations are statements of what you want that you repeat to yourself until you realize your goal. They are clear, so they trigger images to create the results you want. And they are always in affirmative language to sharpen your focus. "I want..." instead of "I don't want..." as we just covered.

The reason they work is because when you hear something enough, you believe it. Just like the things you heard when you were young, you believed them to be true. Even if, and especially when, things in your life aren't the way you want them.

If you pay attention to the most successful people in business, sports or entertainment, you've probably heard their stories of what they did to become successful. Aside from doing the work to master their skill set, they also set their minds on a vision of what they wanted to achieve. Then talked to themselves constantly with affirmations. Once they decided on the goal, they set out telling themselves they could do it, they're a winner, they're going all the way to the top.

If you assume their path was absent of obstacles, you're mistaken. They focused so clearly on the end result that if an obstacle came up, they saw a way to overcome it and kept going. Often times, obstacles that arise are coming from us and our imagination going in a negative, fear-based direction. Therefore, there are also plenty of stories of those who let obstacles stop them. They may have been making excuses or placing blame on people or circumstances for their lack of achievement.

The difference between winning and losing is merely a choice to focus on winning. If you believe you're not a born winner, then change your path right now by saying:

"I'm a winner."

Say it to yourself over and over. If there's something you want, create an affirmation and repeat it over and over. It's most powerful saying it in present tense as if you already have it and are feeling good about having achieved your goal. To get you started, use the following format borrowed from one of the greatest teachers of life success, Bob Proctor:

I'm so happy and grateful now that: _____.

EXERCISE

Choose one of the statements you wrote about in the action step from chapter 5 about things you want. Get a new sheet of paper. State your "want" in present tense and in affirmative language. Then write it ten (10) more times right now or enough times so that you memorize it and could recite it on cue if asked by someone what you want. You can do this for as many items as you like.

However, I encourage you to choose just one item as you go through the book the first time while you're learning and mastering these techniques.

CHAPTER 7

Speak Accurately

Say what you mean and mean what you say. Here's a cliché that's good and useful.

When you speak, do your best to be accurate and true and speak with integrity. The truer you are to your word, the more trust and respect you earn. And the more respect you'll have for yourself. This includes saying "I don't know" if you don't know when asked about something.

Do your best to speak accurately. For example, when talking with a loved one about how they're often late, be accurate and say that. Don't say "you're always late" because that's not accurate and immediately disqualifies the validity of your statement. Saying to them you notice that they are "often late," creates an accurate statement of your experience and a legitimate point for conversation.

Consider that your experience and your perception is just that: Your experience and your perception. You can really only legitimately speak for yourself. For example, when someone asks about an event you attended and what it was like, you might have had a bad experience because something bad happened… for you. However, it's totally possible that everyone else had a great time. So, if you say, "Oh, the event was terrible" then you're not speaking accurately. It could have very well been an exceptionally successful event in every way EXCEPT the things that weren't great for you. An accurate response might sound like, "I was late and missed the opening presentation and my food was overcooked, however the venue was beautiful and everyone looked like they were having a great time."

Remember now that we're looking for winning words and creating a winning life. So, what's an alternative response that could level up your experience and project a better you? You could respond, "It was a successful event" and leave it at that. It's accurate and to the point and you're staying focused on the positive, which is good for you and everyone you engage with.

Winning words, winning life.

EXERCISE

Beginning today, do your best to speak as accurately as possible when answering questions or making any statement. For example: If you're running late to meet a friend and you feel bad and say "I'm just around the corner," when you're actually 15 minutes away, be brave and tell the truth. Say, "I left late and I'm still 15 minutes away, I apologize." You can take it one step further and journal at the end of any day. Here you'll recap conversations you had and make note of as many things you said that you could have said better. Write down those accurate statements to reinforce the habit of re-thinking how you speak.

CHAPTER 8

Let Go of These Words

There are a few words that are problematic when setting yourself up to win. So, let go of them.

BUT – usually states and creates a conflict or contradiction in your sentence. Maybe you've heard that whatever comes after this word negates whatever came before it or reveals a contradiction of two positions. The effect is a weak statement that takes away your power and confidence when you speak and creates a divide. Use the word "AND" instead and watch what happens to your language. You either resolve the conflict or empower the situation by stating the case inclusively.

TRY – Saying you'll try is like having the intention to fail. Remember Yoda in "Star Wars?" He told us, "Do or do not, there is no try." Yes, it's that simple. Even if you say, "I tried that and I suck at it.". Well, you DID DO that thing. If you "tried making the team," the truth is "you DID NOT make the team."

CAN'T – is a useless and defeatist word. Saying you can't do something isn't true. If you didn't do something, you just didn't want it enough to figure out a way to achieve your goal. It's okay, everyone has their own path and goals. Just follow your own path and focus on success. Because you can.

SHOULD – is an interesting way of saying you're not going to do the thing you think you're supposed to do. So, don't say you "should." Either do that thing and say you did, or don't do it and let it go.

WISH – is okay when you're five years old and you're unaware how to make things happen. Now that you're an adult, you're able to make choices and decide what you want and go for your goals. Wishing has no power behind it. Stating your intention and following through with confidence is powerful.

Start now and take one word a day and notice when they come up. Start using different words to express what you mean in a clear, affirmative and powerful way. Start with eliminating "but." You might have to slow down and give more thought before you speak and that's okay. It's better to slow down, do this right and create new winning habits now.

What's great is that you'll actually see how it changes things in your life. You'll get a different response from people when you speak. You'll garner more respect because you're not contradicting yourself and you'll come off more confident.

EXERCISE

Get an index card or small sheet of paper and write down these five words in a column on the left side of the card. Throughout your day, pay attention to your language and make a tally or tic mark every time you speak these words. Do this for one week straight every day and see if you can minimize your use of these words. When you're in the moment, whenever you catch yourself, pause and rephrase the statement in a new way without using that word. You might even be open about it in a conversation and say something like "actually, let me rephrase that..." and then continue with whatever you were saying. For example, BEFORE: "I would love to sing, but I have a terrible voice." AFTER: "I would love to sing **and** I'm sure voice lessons would help."

It's such a
CLICHÉ

CHAPTER 9

Rethink Clichés

Clichés are statements that were created at some point in time when they may have been relevant. They are then are borrowed and used by others. Sometimes they fit and sometimes they're used incorrectly. These phrases are overused and tired. Even if they fit, it's better to come up with original thoughts and speak your own words.

For example, some say "age breeds wisdom" and there are a lot of senior folks who are not wise at all. What actually breeds wisdom is experience and learning from those experiences. Some people learn better than others, so you can be young and wise. In this example, you can see how going along with an old statement is limiting.

Another example is "that's the way the cookie crumbles." This is meant to be a statement of acceptance when something goes wrong, suggesting that the outcome was destined to be a certain way because "that's the way the cookie crumbles." Actually, that's the way THAT cookie crumbled. The way THAT situation worked out. It's actually a victim statement disguised as some quick wit attitude.

Just be aware of what you pick up from others and whether it even makes sense or applies in your conversations and speech. Consider whether these sayings and clichés are empowering you or limiting you.

Think for yourself and come up with your own unique ideas and perspectives; choose your own words to state them. Be a leader in thought and speech, and pave a new path. Your winning path.

Let go of clichés and allow your mind to expand and be creative in finding new ways to say what you mean. When your mind expands and your vocabulary expands, so does your world. Choose new and winning words for your new and winning life.

And if you really like clichés, use this one:

"Say what you mean, and mean what you say."

And follow this simple advice:

"Think for yourself."

EXERCISE

Get a sheet of paper. Draw a vertical line down the middle. On the left side, write out ten (10) cliches that you're familiar with and use often or hear other people use often. On the right side, think of a new way to say the same thing using different words. Write that down for you to use going forward. Example: OLD: "I've been banging my head against a brick wall." NEW: "I'm committed to figuring this out."

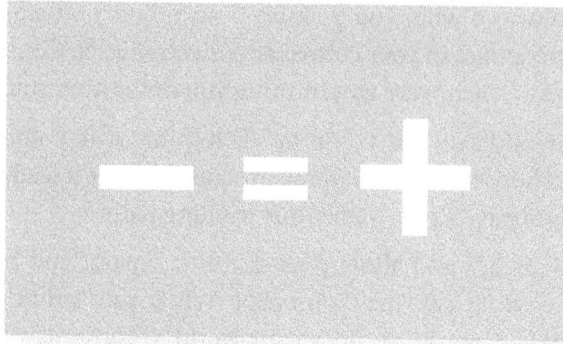

CHAPTER 10

Less is More

An important way to improve the quality of your speech is by using fewer words to make your point. Think of the 30 second elevator speech we all talk about. The most successful people know how to get their point across clearly with fewer words.

This is achieved by being clear on your objective, knowing your audience and choosing the best approach. In social and business situations, it's always worth the effort to be concise and choose your words wisely to contribute to the conversation in the best possible way.

The most successful people know how to add value, be precise and leave room for others to shine. They listen and learn from others how to best come into the conversation with value.

Be confident and let go of the need to explain yourself, validate your argument, defend your position and prove you're right. Answer questions with fewer words and provide details when people ask for more.

Fun Fact: Some people offer more detail than they actually know for sure. It's almost a reflex, however it does come from a good place. Our brain actually fills in details to complete memories when we don't remember everything. This is because our brains want to complete open loops. It's a survival technique. We're relying on our ability to categorize details of events in order to judge our level of safety. Our brain is literally functioning to protect us.

However, we can be fooled by perception so sometimes we actually remember things wrong. Beware of people who are overly confident in the extreme detail of something that proves them right. And don't be that person. Be open to the possibility that you have some information and that by conversing with someone else, you can put the pieces together and find the truth. In reality, there are far fewer things that you know fully than you initially think. Remember to be truthful and say "I don't know" when that's the case.

Again, this shows integrity, humility and trustworthiness. When you really, truly know something, people will see it and know and trust you because you've set a standard of integrity.

Your word is your bond. Your honor. Be selective and choose truth and harmony. You win and so does everyone else.

EXERCISE

In your conversations, practice answering questions that you are asked with a single sentence as a statement of facts. Do your best to omit opinion, explanations, tangents and extra information. In this exercise, the objective is to make a clear point first. Then if someone asks for your opinion or explanation or additional information, you repeat the exercise and respond with a single sentence as concisely as possible. The objective is to think about the best way to get your point across if you just have a few seconds.

CHAPTER 11

Value Over Volume

"People don't care what you know until they know you care."

– Theodore Roosevelt

Certain people talk in a way that makes you hang on their words and enjoy hearing what they have to say. What they have to say has value.

Opposite of this, there are some people who talk without much value to the extent that you might want to tune them out. What's worse is they may talk over everyone else to be in control of the conversation and the center of attention.

If in this second scenario, the person could just realize if they had something of value to say to their audience, everyone would be begging for their opinion instead of them having to force it on everyone.

They could be like the first person to speak of things that are relevant and valuable to their audience. Once they're focused on the audience, people would start to pay attention.

You start by listening to people, listening to what they care about so you know how to contribute to a conversation that improves the quality of time together and adds value to that person's life. It's more than just talking or noise or filling the silence.

People will seek you out, they'll look up to you, they'll be influenced by you, they'll care about you and what you have to say because you add value to their lives.

When you study the most successful business people, you'll see they understand and practice this. They get the best referrals because people have a great experience with them and are truly enriched by the relationship. Then people talk to their friends and associates about this person in the best possible light.

Keep in mind that these are ways of being with people in conversation and how you speak that are actionable items. And to really truly be the winner is to really truly care about others. This must not be an act for winning sake. That's not sincere. That's not cool. Be cool. Be genuine. Think of people who care about you and how you're motivated to care for them in return. So be like that. You care first. You give first. Listen and learn how to be more valuable in your circle. Let go of the need to win arguments and you'll gain your winning life.

EXERCISE

In your next conversations, do your best to listen first and pay attention to what matters most to the people involved in the conversation. Be patient to speak and when you do speak, say something that encompasses the essence of the conversation as a statement of your understanding what matters to the group. Put it in an inclusive and positive statement that benefits everyone.

I/We

CHAPTER 12

Speaking in First Person

Speak for yourself!

Speaking in first person means speaking from personal experience and using "I am" or "I think" or "I feel." It's good to know what it is, the value of it and why it's important.

You can only really speak with integrity when speaking from personal experience and using the word "I" when offering perspective. You were there and you had an experience. You have your perspective and opinion about that experience or that thing or that person. No one else can speak more truthfully on your behalf than you. And others can speak of their life experience better than you can.

Now you're responsible for your words about you and your life experience. You're saying "I am," "I think," "I feel," "I believe" and "I want" and so on. Incorporating everything we've covered so far actually puts you in a really powerful position by applying all the principles. Because all your words are focusing on the positive of what you WANT, they're original thoughts and words, they're truthful, they're valuable and they're intentionally selected to be clear and succinct.

You're also vulnerable because you're expressing yourself wholly and truthfully and now it means something. You're owning all of it. That shows maturity, confidence and responsibility. Be sure to speak using "I" statements. "I am a winner," "I feel," "I want," "I will."

If there's a conversation that comes up about a subject that you have no experience with, simply listen and learn from others. If the subject was brought up, that probably means there's someone there who has actual experience and feelings about it who can expand your perspective if you choose to speak on it at some later point.

Consider a scenario in which you and your friend are in a group conversation and something comes up that's awkward for you, so you make a joke to alleviate the tension. The conversation ends, the group disperses and you say to your friend, "That was awkward!" Well, actually, it was awkward for YOU. It's out of line to speak for everyone. Say instead, "I felt awkward there" to speak from personal experience.

Integrity, responsibility and honesty are all winning qualities. Be a winner.

EXERCISE

Get a sheet of paper and make a list of 10 or subjects that you're an expert in, have a lot experience with or have strong feelings about that you could stand up for with confidence if met with challenge from another. Then see if you can commit to mostly only speaking up when it comes to these matters and using statements like "In my experience...." and "I've seen..." and "I did..." and "I like...." When it comes to subjects that are outside your wheelhouse, focus on being curious and learning about new things while being slow to speak about things that are out of your expertise.

You/Your

CHAPTER 13

Speaking in the Second Person

Speaking in the second person is speaking to someone using words like "you," "your," and "you're." Let's consider the best ways to speak to someone in your winning life.

Remember that your words are powerful as they trigger images, which trigger results. And remember how you were influenced by your family and community as a result of what they said to you about you. If they were encouraging and positive, saying such things as "You're awesome!" and "You're a good kid," and "You can do it," well, that's what you accepted and believed and acted out. Negative statements that were spoken had the same effect in influencing you.

Speaking negatively and being critical is hurtful and damaging to any relationship. It's de-motivating whether you're speaking to a loved one or business associate or teammate. There are people who use fear tactics for motivating and controlling people, and it works sometimes. However, it's usually short-lived and leads to a worse situation in the long run and sometimes irreversible pain.

So, focusing on the positive and speaking positively to others is the best way to go. Be a leader and be empowering. Consider appropriate expressions for the best possible outcome. Be confident enough in yourself to build up others. Most people appreciate and respect you for it and will consider you a leader, a good friend and so on. And if they don't, it's okay. They might be distracted or unaware of the value you provide in their life. Just accept them for who they are and keep doing the right thing.

As much as possible, when saying a "You are…" type phrase to someone, say something positive and be sincere. "You are so helpful." "You're a great cook." "You're a good friend." "You're awesome!" If you don't have anything positive to say, don't say anything. Just be cool, be respectful, accept them and let them be.

Focus on winning words and your winning life. This includes good relationships.

EXERCISE

In your conversations, find a way to do two things: 1 – compliment the person to whom your speaking on one specific thing about them personally. 2 – Thank them for something specific. Example: "Thank you for making time to meet for coffee. I appreciate how you seek to serve your community by teaching others what you know about financial investments."

He/She/They

CHAPTER 14

Speaking in the Third Person

"Great minds discuss ideas; average minds discuss events; small minds discuss people."

– Eleanor Roosevelt

Speaking in the third person is when you're talking to someone about someone else using the words "he," "she," or "they."

There are times when you must speak about someone outside their presence and in your winning life. When this is the case, use words in a positive light and uplift them like "They're awesome."

Be aware of your words, consider whether they're really necessary, are from personal experience and are improving the situation. Remember it's best to be responsible and speak with integrity, speaking only for yourself of your personal experience with that person. Discussing what someone else thinks about someone isn't really your place. Even if you're just repeating what's been said, it's basically gossip. And that's not winning.

Sometimes people get caught up in situations when someone asks them for information and it might feel normal to just answer the question. Maybe someone asks you, "Are they mad at me?" And maybe you know the answer is yes. However, if you answer "Yes, they're mad at you because you did that thing and they're upset and it caused them to..." and so on with details, then you're allowing drama to stir up and the problem isn't getting solved. A more productive response would be "Ask them. They can speak for themselves better than I can." This shows respect for both parties and maintains your integrity.

An example where it's appropriate to talk about someone else would be giving a referral for business or making new friends. If someone is looking for a good assistant, you can talk about someone you know and say something like, "I know someone who might be a good assistant. They're smart, responsible and organized. I like them, you might too." Or if you're connecting new friends, you might say, "Hey, I made a friend at the gym and they like live music too. I enjoy their company and they're super nice. Let's go out sometime and see how it goes."

Be the person that's making situations and conversations better, not worse. And if you have nothing good to say about someone, don't say anything. Be cool.

Choose a winning style with winning attitude and winning words.

EXERCISE

In your next conversations, when someone's name comes up and that person isn't there to speak for themselves, work something positive into the conversation about them. If the conversation is negative about a specific person, do your best to redirect the conversation to something neutral or positive about that person or something else altogether. Do your best to refrain from participating in perpetuation of anything negative about someone else.

CHAPTER 15

Act as If

You've probably heard this before and it works. So it's worth looking at why it's so powerful.

Acting as if you already have the thing you want, puts you in a state of mind that keeps the image of your end result resonating even stronger within you so you achieve your goal faster.

Act as if you have the thing you want or you are who you want to be while you do the things outlined in this book. Both need to happen.

For example, let's say you want to double your income. Let's say that would allow you a significantly more comfortable lifestyle than right now. Maybe right now you don't do things because you think you can't afford it or maybe even struggle to pay your bills. Your current circumstances probably come with feelings of stress and anxiety.

The opposite of that scenario, in which you have double the money, would likely feel calm and confident and you'd probably enjoy nicer things or take trips. So, you might not literally have the money in your bank account instantly, however acting like you have the money you want, acting calm and confident, keeps your focus on taking the steps to achieve the new reality. And funny thing, speaking from experience, is that people and circumstances will start to show up differently for you to move you closer to your goal and very quickly when you act as if it's already true!

Think about your winning words to match your winning act. For example, in the present moment you might not have the money you want or need. A friend might ask how you are and how things are going. In the old reality, you might tell them all your money problems and talk about how stressed you are and why. However, remember what all those words do. Talking about your money problems makes you think of them more. It triggers images of struggle and worry and magnifies that picture to perpetuate that pattern. So, instead, say, "I'm good! How are you?" Stay focused on the positive and keep acting in faith that you're taking the right steps in the right direction toward earning more money and achieving your other goals.

Think and imagine and feel and act as the person you want to be having what you want.

Live your winning life.

EXERCISE

Get a sheet of paper and draw a vertical line down the middle. Refer to the list you made during Chapter 5 when you made a list of things you want and choose your three favorite things or top priorities. On the new sheet of paper, one at a time, rewrite the three top things in a question form of "How will it FEEL when I...?" on the left side. Then answer your question on the right side with feeling words. For example: "I will feel happy, grateful, fulfilled, free and energized!" Then focus on these FEELING WORDS as you go about your day. Feeling the feelings of already having what you want will bring what you want faster.

CHAPTER 16

Inside Out

Real and lasting change comes when what's going on inside you reflects the new and winning you: when you've formed new habits, when these winning ways are normal and automatic for you.

You automatically think and speak to yourself in winning ways. You've made a new and good habit of keeping images of your positive end result in mind until you achieve your goal. You focus on what you want, not what you don't want. You use affirmations to stay focused. You've let go of counterproductive vocabulary. You've let go of clichés and have unique thoughts and express them in new and creative ways. You speak truthfully and offer value, using as few words as possible to deliver your message. You speak for yourself, you speak to others in ways that are uplifting and encouraging, and speak of others in a positive light.

To help form new habits, it's good to invest additional effort into each point highlighted in these chapters. Maybe take one chapter each day and focus on that one concept or objective. This book was designed as a quick and easy read, however, some need reinforcement depending on learning style or personality. Consider some of the following.

Keep a journal and make notes on what you've read and your ideas about it. You probably have life experiences similar to the examples offered here so you can apply the principles to your situation and tailor it to fit you specifically. For example, if there's something you want, write it out in specific detail while focusing on the end result. Stay focused on the good stuff. The positive details. The benefits. Or if there's someone that bothers you, take time to write out their positive aspects and practice speaking of others in a positive light even if they're not your best friend.

Take one day at a time and practice one chapter or one concept at a time. For example, one day focus on speaking to others with empowering language by saying something positive like, "Thanks for helping me the other day, I feel grateful for our friendship."

Spend time in meditation or prayer. Clear your mind, focus and visualize your winning life in detail. Or spend time thinking of things you're grateful for so the images play out over and over and magnify the good in your life.

Internalize your winning life in your winning way. Do what works for you. Choose winning.

EXERCISE

Get a sheet of paper and make a list of as many wins as you can think of in the last week. These could be things you accomplished or things that happened that you appreciate. The point is to create a habit of positive focus so your thoughts, words and actions are geared towards winning. All progress is success and deserves acknowledgement. Appreciating each win brings more. Do this daily or as often as possible.

*Tomorrow
I will...*

CHAPTER 17

Walk Your Talk

"Actions speak louder than words."

– Unknown

Let's make sure your actions match your new words because while you're making efforts to change your language, people are still paying attention to what you do.

If you say, "I'm going to pick you up at 6," then be there at 6. When your words and actions match, your integrity is intact and you're earning the respect and trust of those who matter. And soon, it won't be a matter of IF you'll follow through on what you said, it's just assumed you will. Your word truly becomes your bond.

There are plenty of people who say one thing and do another. That affects people more than you realize. It also hurts feelings and strains relationships. And none of these are winning qualities of life. So, be aware of things you say, make sure you're speaking with integrity and are committed to honoring your word.

Even with the best of intentions, you might find you're not able to do what you've promised. You might have been telling your friend you're going to sign up for the gym with them so you can work out together. Maybe you've been saying this for awhile without following through. Consider being honest and say something like, "I want to join your gym... however, my budget's already allocated for" or "I prefer going in the afternoon."

People usually appreciate honesty even when you think they won't. The fears are usually coming from inside you. You might feel guilty that you don't have the same goals. Or maybe you have a fear of missing out. Whatever the reason for saying yes, when the action is a no... do your best going forward to match your walk with your talk.

Walk the talk, or change your talk to match the path you're willing to walk.

It takes a certain amount of bravery to say no and admit mistakes and miscalculation. And that bravery you muster to match the walk to the talk builds self-esteem and self-respect. You're actually demonstrating respect for others when you're honest with them, earning their respect in turn. It's good all around.

More of your winning life will emerge as you walk your talk.

EXERCISE

Get a sheet of paper and at the top write the words: "Tomorrow I will..." and then list three things you want to accomplish the next day. Be sure you accomplish those three things and check them off your list. Using the words "I will..." and then following through is powerful. If the exercise was easy, then scale up to five things. If it was challenging, then scale down to one or two items so you can be in integrity. If you want to take it one step further, for everything you did on the list, write a statement like "I said I was going to.... and I did."

CHAPTER 18

Other People's Words

Awareness of your own words and how they affect you brings to light others' words also.

Reading this material might have triggered a new understanding of how conversations in your past have affected you. Maybe some conversations from your childhood. Maybe a conversation yesterday with a loved one.

Whether these memories are positive or negative, you can still appreciate the lessons learned about how words have affected you. You can focus on your new understanding and power to create your winning life. Stay on track no matter what, including when others' words are not winning and not in your best interest.

Sometimes, even good-hearted people with good intentions can unintentionally oppose your success. For example, say you set a goal for yourself and you tell a friend about it. If they have limiting beliefs, you might be talked out of your dream by the end of that conversation. Not because they don't love you or want you to succeed though. They might just have fears and insecurities that limit their thinking. In this case, they're unintentionally projecting them onto you, wanting to protect you by pointing out everything that could go wrong. They don't want you to face disappointment so they draw an elaborate picture of the worst case scenario. Remember the ski trip example? Sometimes you talk yourself out of things and sometimes others talk you out of things that could be good for you.

So, focus on what you want, on reinforcing your affirmative and winning words and images as much as possible so your confidence overrides anything negative that comes at you. You want to be so sure of yourself, so clear in your vision of your goals and be walking your talk so confidently that when someone intentionally or unintentionally comes at you with less than winning words, you're able to say something like, "Thanks for sharing your perspective." Then redirect the conversation to a neutral subject or something positive about them. You might even find that you need to be selective of the people you share your dreams with. Or who you spend your time with in general. If someone is mostly negative or toxic, it's okay to take care of yourself by setting yourself apart from them and finding people more in alignment with your path of success. Find winners to associate with.

Being a winner with a winning life includes winning relationships and conversations.

Exercise

In your next conversations, pay attention to how others speak and whether or not they're success-oriented. Also note that many leaders and teachers of success agree that we are the sum of the five people with whom we spend the most time. So consider the relationships in your life, how they influence you, and whether you can to improve the quality of your relationships and how you invest your time in them.

CHAPTER 19

Listen and Learn

Listening is a skill and as important a part of communication as speech is.

You can learn a lot from listening to others and paying attention to their life situation. This is true whether you're studying very successful people or those who often struggle.

Think of our previous examples of people who overcame obstacles to reach their success. Be aware of successful people you meet, hear about or see on TV and notice how they speak. Their language often highlights their achievements and positively focuses on future goals. They're often speaking in terms of being grateful and appreciative of others who've contributed to their success. Their language is uplifting and inspiring. Note that some people are successful in some areas of life and not others. Some people may even be negative or harsh even with all their success. Those are not the examples you want to follow. You want to follow the superpowers in their field. The greatest leaders. The ones who are loved and admired across industry lines, across generations, to a wide audience.

Also, notice people who are negative or down on themselves and others and how it relates to the results they produce. Listen and learn from them as well. You might notice things they do that you used to do, which will reinforce what you've learned and encourage you to keep moving in this positive direction. Or, maybe you'll notice things they do that haven't been a limitation of yours. Being aware of allows you to sidestep those pitfalls in the future. Either way, you can always learn from people and experiences when you're open.

In addition to listening and studying others' speech as a way of expanding your awareness, it's also good to listen to what matters to others, what they want and what motivates them. This is valuable when making connections with people and allows you to be a better leader, better friend, better teammate.

For example, when you listen with the intention of understanding people better, you might notice they often talk about wanting to learn to play golf and notice they haven't in years. You can be a supportive friend and say something like, "Hey, I notice you get excited when you talk about golf. And you've also said you want more work-life balance. Maybe taking up golf could be a way to achieve that goal. And it'd be fun!"

A winning life includes listening to others, learning from others, giving to others and serving others.

Exercise

Make a list of 10 successful people you admire. If you're interested in a specific niche or market as a business or hobby, you may want to just focus on people in that area. Whatever you choose, the next step is to make a list of words that describes them. For example, you find your favorite people to be smart and inspiring and generous. Study them further and take one page of notes on why they're successful. Now go back to the chapter on affirmations and write one page of affirmations for yourself to use on a daily basis while imagining yourself embodying those qualities.

CHAPTER 20

Live and Let Live

As you discover your winning life, you might feel like telling others they need to also.

You've become aware of these concepts and have been applying them and finding great success as a result. You care about your loved ones and want great success for them as well. Therefore, it's natural to want to share everything you've learned, what you're doing and how great it's been. So, do that and do your best to leave it there.

Even though I love this material and want to reach as many people as possible, I believe it's best to lead by example. Find your mastery in this work and let your success speak for you. Let your winning ways show others how things can improve in life by applying these methods.

Telling someone how they can change and how life can be better may come off as telling them that how they're currently living is somehow wrong or not good enough –maybe even that you think THEY aren't good enough the way they are.

Even in cases when someone is clearly down on themselves or self-destructive, they may be unaware and unable to hear your well-intentioned message. They might outright disagree. This creates a divide and hurts the communication lines in relationships.

Respect the fact that everyone has their own path and others may or may not agree with or understand your choices. Not everyone wants the same things. And that's okay!

Sometimes people are even tense when someone they know moves to new heights of success. It's usually unconscious and comes from a place of having a different rhythm in communication and lifestyle. It's new and foreign and therefore sometimes uncomfortable. That's okay too! As people grow and change, they have to get used to the changes and there's sometimes an adjustment period. Just go with it and be cool.

Be kind, respectful and compassionate. Be encouraging, uplifting and inspiring.

The best way to influence your loved ones is by example. Live and let live.

Simply live your winning life.

Exercise

Consider incorporating the following affirmation into your daily routine: "Everyone has free will to live as they choose, as do I." Since this statement is true, I offered it here as something to consider. And if there's a better way to state the same idea that resonates better for you, please consider crafting that statement accordingly and consider incorporating it into your daily routine.

ABOUT THE AUTHOR

Victoria Draper earned her Bachelor of Arts in Rhetoric & Communication from the University of California at Davis and has continued her fascination and study of the language choices used by the most successful people in the world. As an entrepreneur, athlete and coach, Victoria has first-hand experience in understanding the correlation between our word choices and the impact it has on achieving success in life.

Victoria has created multiple start-up companies focused in the areas of fitness, online marketing and personal development. In addition to leading her own organization, Victoria currently serves as a speaker, mentor, consultant and expert contributor in the fields of business, entrepreneurship and online marketing.

Her accomplishments and expert insight has been featured in many publications including *Newsweek, Shape Magazine, Max Fitness* and *Sunset* lifestyle magazine. She also served as the rowing consultant for the competitors on NBC's *Biggest Loser* fitness show.

The inspiration for this book came from her desire to simplify the path to success and personal fulfillment by consolidating these ideas and to share the methods she uses with her clients. This book is the manifestation of her mission and desire to share her insight, tips and tools for crafting Winning Words into the Winning Life for everyone seeking to enhance their life mastery skills.

To find out more about Victoria and
Winning Words, Winning Life,
please visit the following websites

winningwordswinninglife.com

To purchase the book please go to amazon.com

Facebook: Victoria Draper

Instagram: thewinningmethod

Email: Victoria@winningwordswinninglife.com

HEARTS to be HEARD

Giving a Voice to Creativity!

Wouldn't you love to help the physically, spiritually,
and mentally challenged?

Would you like to make a difference
in a child's life?

Imagine giving them:
confidence; self-esteem; pride; and self-respect.
Perhaps a legacy that lives on.

You see, that's what we do.
We give a voice to the creativity in their hearts,
for those who would otherwise not be heard.

Join us by going to
HeartstobeHeard.com
Help us, help others.

www.ingramcontent.com/pod-product-compliance
Lightning Source LLC
Chambersburg PA
CBHW071336200326
41520CB00013B/3009